PROPHET YUNUS STORY

Maison
Blue

A long long time ago, there was a city named Nineveh. The people of Nineveh were idolaters, who lived a shameless life. Prophet Yunus peace be upon him was sent by Allah to Nineveh, to preach to them about the true God.

"You should believe only in Allah and obey his commands" He told them, "Otherwise a severe punishment will come upon you" He warned them.

But the inhabitants of the town didn't like anyone to interfere in their way of worship.

"We and our forefathers have worshipped these Gods for many years" said an old man.

"And no harm has come to us" added another.

Prophet Yunus peace be upon him tried very hard to convince the people about Allah . But the people kept ignoring him He warned that if they kept on with their foolishness, Allah will soon punish them.

Instead of fearing Allah, they told the Prophet that they were not afraid of his threats.

"Let your God punish us" they told him.

The Prophet was disheartened by now.

"In that case I will leave you to your misery" saying that, he leftthe town of Nineveh.   The   Prophet   became impatient and he departed without waiting for further commands from Allah. He knew that God must be angry on him, so he decided to travel to a distant land.

As soon as the Prophet left the city, the skies began to change its color. It looked like they were on fire! The people were filled by fear at this sight! They remembered the destruction of the people of Aad, Thamud and Nuh! Slowly faith started penetrating their hearts. The people of Nineveh gathered on the top of a mountain, and started to pray to Allah for His mercy. The mountains echoed with their cries, the people of Nineveh repented sincerely for the sins they had committed. When Allah heard their prayers, he decided not to punish them, and He showered His blessing upon the people once again! When

the people realized that they were saved, they prayed to Allah for the return of Yunus peace be upon him, so that he could guide them.

Meanwhile, Yunus peace be upon him had boarded a small ship in the company of other passengers.

It sailed all day in calm waters, with a good wind blowing at the sails. But as the night came, the sea suddenly changed. There was a horrible storm, and it looked like the ship was going to be split into pieces! The waves rose as high as mountains, tossing the ship up and down! Everyone in the ship were terrified!

The captain of the ship shouted to the crew to lighten the ships heavy load. The crew first threw their baggage overboard, but this was not enough! Their safety lay in reducing the weight further, so they decided among themselves, that one among them will have to be thrown into the sea.

In the meantime, a large whale had surfaced behind the ship. Allah had commanded the whale to surface, and it had obeyed. The whale kept following the ship as he had been commanded.

And back at the ship, the captain told them "We will make lots with all the

travelers names. The one whose name is drawn will be thrown into the sea."

Yunus Peace be upon him reluctantly participated in the lot, and his name was added as well. When the lot was drawn, the paper had "Yunus" written

on it!

Since the crew knew that the Prophet was the most honorable man among them, they didn't want to throw him into the sea. Therefore they decided to draw a second lot. And when they drew the lot for the second time, the name of the Prophet appeared again!! The crew decided to give one final chance to the Prophet, and drew a third lot. But the Prophet's name appeared during the third and final lot as well! The Prophet realized that Allah was involved in what was going on. He realized that Allah was punishing him, because he had abandoned the mission without Allah's consent. It was decided that the Prophet should throw himself into the water. Yunus peace be up on him stood at the edge of the ship, looking at the furious sea. It was night and there was no moon in the sky. The stars were hidden behind a black fog. Before jumping into the sea, the Prophet kept mentioning Allah's name. He then jumped into the sea, and disappeared beneath the huge waves. The whale that was following the ship, found the Prophet floating on the waves. It didn't waste anytime, and swallowed the Prophet in one gulp! The whale shut its ivory teeth, as if they were white bolts locking the door of his prison. It then dived to the bottom of the sea.

The Prophet imagined himself to be dead, but his senses became alert when he figured that he was able to on it!

Since the crew knew that the Prophet was the most honorable man among them, they didn't want to throw him into the sea. Therefore they decided to draw a second lot. And when they drew the lot for the second time, the name of the Prophet appeared again!! The crew decided to give one final chance to the Prophet, and drew a third lot. But the Prophet's name appeared during the third and final lot as well! The Prophet realized that Allah was involved in what was going on. He realized that Allah was punishing him, because he had abandoned the mission without Allah's consent. It was decided that the Prophet should throw himself into the water. Yunus peace be up on him stood at the edge of the ship, looking at the furious sea. It was night and there was no moon in the sky. The stars were hidden behind a black fog. Before jumping into the sea, the Prophet kept mentioning Allah's name. He then jumped into the sea, and disappeared beneath the huge waves. The whale that was following the ship, found the Prophet floating on the waves. It didn't waste anytime, and swallowed the Prophet in one gulp! The whale shut its ivory teeth, as if they were white bolts locking the door of his prison. It then dived to the bottom of the sea.

The Prophet imagined himself to be dead, but his senses became alert when he figured that he was able to

move. He realized that he was alive, and knew that he was imprisoned. In his loneliness, he started to think over what had happened in the town, and realized that he should have never left the town. Instead, he should have stayed and kept on speaking to the people, asking them to return to Allah In his despair, the Prophet started to pray with all his heart to Allah.

 "O Allah, there is no God apart from You. You alone do I praise and honor.
I have done wrong, if You do not help me, I shall be lost for ever" The Prophet continued praying to Allah, repeating his prayers.

Fishes, whales and many other creatures that lived in the sea, heard the voice of the Prophet's prayers,

coming from the whale's stomach All these creatures gathered around the whale, and began to praise Allah, each in its own language!! The whale also participated in praising Allah. Then he understood that he had swallowed a Prophet! When he realized this, He felt afraid at first! He then said to himself "Why should I be afraid? Allah commanded me to swallow him" Allah Almighty saw the sincere repentance of the Prophet, and He decided to save him! He commanded the whale to go the surface, and eject the Prophet onto the shore.

The whale obeyed and swam to the surface of the ocean. He then ejected the Prophet onto a remote island!

The Prophet was very sick now because of the acids inside the whale's stomach. His skin was inflamed, and when the sun rose, the rays burned his body! The Prophet was on the verge of screaming with pain by now. But he endured the pain and continued his prayers to Allah.

Allah then, caused a tree to grow behind where the Prophet was praying. This tree protected the Prophet from the harsh rays of the sun, and it gave him nourishing fruits as well! Gradually, he regained his strength and found his way back to Nineveh.

He was pleasantly surprised to notice the change that took place!

The entire population of Nineveh turned out to welcome him!! They informed him that they now worshipped Allah, the one true God.

The Prophet was very happy to hear that, And he lived happily in Nineveh until he died!

THANK
YOU